THE REASON LOVE REACHES

POEMS FOR LENT / SAM GUTIERREZ

THE REASON LOVE REACHES

POEMS FOR LENT / SAM GUTIERREZ

Lent Scripture Verses

Blow the trumpet in Zion;
sound the alarm on my holy
hill... "Even now," declares the
LORD, "Return to me with all
your heart, with fasting and
weeping and mourning."
Rend your heart and not your
garments. Return to the
LORD your God, for he is
gracious and compassionate,
slow to anger and abounding
in love, and he relents from
sending calamity.

Joel 2:12-13

Have mercy on me, O God,
according to your unfailing
love; according to your great
compassion blot out my
transgressions. Wash away all
my iniquity and cleanse me
from my sin.

Psalm 51:1-2

Doesn't he leave the ninety-
nine in the open country and
go after the lost sheep until he
finds it?

Luke 15:4

When he came to his senses…
he got up and went to his
father.

Luke 15:20

Introduction

One of my favorite hymns
was written over 250 years ago
by Robert Robinson. In middle
of the fourth verse, seven little
words summarize the strong
and strange inclination of every
human heart - *prone to wander,
Lord, I feel it.*

Lent is a 40-day season in the
church calendar that calls us to
name all the ways we wander –
some obvious, some subtle.
Then, to turn towards the God
who loves us and has been
eagerly waiting for our return.

Not only does God patiently
wait for us to turn toward
home, God actively goes out
and searches for us.

The reason love reaches so far
into the darkness to find us and
bring us back is hard to fully
understand. The Bible simply
says - *for God so loved the world.*

These poems are meditations
on scripture that hope to steady
your footsteps as you journey
your way home.

May God bless you richly,

Sam Gutierrez

THE REASON LOVE REACHES

Day 1 / Ash Wednesday

Savior, soak up sin that
stains our skin, smears our
soul, steals our strength and
soils with sadness deep, so
deep.

Psalm 51:1-6

Day 2 / Thursday

Forget fasting. Don't waste
time weeping. All that by itself
is a bunch of baloney. If your
sorry is sincere then show it
by sharing your sandwich with
some poor soul suffering from
stomach ache. That kind
of baloney is the real deal.

Isaiah 58:5-7

Day 3 / Friday

Heaven's favor is a renewable
resource. Your eye is a solar
panel buzzing with brilliance,
your spirit is a windmill
humming with delight,
your heart is a waterwheel
brimming with grace. Love is
energy abundant and
streaming.

2 Corinthians 5:20b-6:2

Day 4 / Saturday

The ego is hungry
for human applause.
The best way to starve
the thing istoblendin.

Matthew 6:16-21

Sunday / 1

To heal the hell
and mend the break
God tolled the knell
to heel the snake.

Then sin did swell
with speed and weight
and struck the Christ
with dread and ache.

Genesis 3:1-7

Day 5 / Monday

No dark corner or dingy
cleft in God. No junk in the
drawer, skeleton in the closet
or crumb under the cushion.
In God, light floods dazzling
light through every nook and
cranny.

1 John 1:5-10

Day 6 / Tuesday

When silence, solitude and
starvation sufficiently sow a
seed of suspicion, the serpent
then strikes with a silvery
song of substantiation.

Matthew 4:1-11

Day 7 / Wednesday

This stain so severe
is stubborn and resurfaces
with resilience. Water will
work for a while but some
solution stronger will be
required to resolve this
stain, so severe.

Genesis 9:8-17

Day 8 / Thursday

One conviction, Christ alive.
One confession, Christ above.
One consolation, Christ beside.
One confidence, Christ below.
One contemplation, Christ within.

Romans 10:9-13

Day 9 / Friday

God's been preparing
a larger than life reunion
party that heaven and earth
have been longing for
since Adam and Eve.

So make plans now
to show or you'll miss seeing
normally serene seraphim
swinging from the
chandeliers.

1 Timothy 2:1-6a

Day 10 / Saturday

When the last drop
disappears remember –
God forever sees you
sopping wet with favor.

1 Peter 3:18-22

Sunday / 2

As you age your vision
improves. Don't tell the young
people that you can now see
around corners - they'll think
you're nuts. Clearly though
you see just around that last
bend is a whole new country.

Genesis 12:1-4

Day 11 / Monday

Eye aches for that gleam
and glimmer but heart tires of
gold and every other precious
thing. Forget about all that
flash and follow me –

I'll show you treasure
worth a serious
obsession.

Genesis 15:1-5

Day 12 / Tuesday

A single seed changed heaven
and earth when God breathed.
A single seed to pass down
blessing like dominos.

Genesis 17:1-7

Day 13 / Wednesday

God graciously gives gifts to
those through trust hold him
happily hostage.

Romans 4:1-5

Day 14 / Thursday

Heaven's golden gate is
where many make a case for
measured morality.

Forget the front and forage
around until you find the back
door. It will be locked but
don't worry or knock, just
kneel and say the Name.

Romans 4:13-17

Day 15 / Friday

Parts fail but God can
take a busted container and
a weathered hose and get
them working like parts fresh
from the factory.

Romans 4:18-25

Day 16 / Saturday

Here comes slip sliding
out of heaven's womb
another beloved child
goopy with grace.

John 3:1-8

Sunday / 3

When Moses struck rock
from the stone came flowing
streams of filtered water –
a refreshing drink
everyone could swallow.

When soldiers struck Christ
from his side came flowing
streams of water and blood –
a redemptive drink
some couldn't stomach.

Exodus 17:1-7

Day 17 / Monday

Ten super high hurdles - stop
and search for a substitute
with that specialized skill set.
See your stand in sail over
those high hurdles no sweat.
Then see him stumble and
suffer so.

Exodus 20:1-17

Day 18 / Tuesday

Every moment unaware of
love we wander in a strange
land, starving.

1 Corinthians 10:1-5, 11-13

Day 19 / Wednesday

Soldiers stormed and tore
him apart brick by brick.
Tumbling temple collapsed
into a bleeding pile of rubble.
In the middle of night God
rolled up his sleeves and
quietly resurrected a house of
radiant flesh and bone.

John 2:13-22

Day 20 / Thursday

Death - don't dish
out heavenly happenings or
earthly equations. Simply,
strangely – earth shivers and
towers shower
b
r
i
c
k
s

on you
and me.

Luke 13:1-9

Day 21 / Friday

Water will splash your soul
awake and start you on the
path. Milk will coat your heart
warmly and quiet you on the
way. Wine will work your hips
loose and whirl you to
wild rhythms.

Isaiah 55:1-3, 6-7

Day 22 / Saturday

God was glad when God
had some time to tackle
some things on his
to-do list like –

disarming death.

Romans 5:6-11

Sunday / 4

Look down –
sin strikes and venom surges
through your veins threatening
your heart to black.

Look up –
sin hangs nailed to a pole
oozing precious antidote.

Numbers 21:4-9

Day 23 / Monday

In a region
beyond the rational –

the reason love reaches

John 3:14-21

Day 24 / Tuesday

Sinners pray like this:
stand at a distance,
stare at the ground,
strike steady your heart,
say – Lord have mercy.

Luke 18:9-14

Day 25 / Wednesday

Wealth requires sound advice.
Worldly wisdom said diversify,
but angels sing one risky
enterprise that paid
dividends profound.

Ephesians 2:1-10

Day 26 / Thursday

Evil is a pair of empty hands –
don't be a tool.

Romans 6:8-14

Day 27 / Friday

Inhale – Life,
Exhale – Death,
Inhale – Resurrection.

Practice daily.

Mark 8:34-38

Day 28 / Saturday

Wake up,
Christ is shining on you.
Everything illuminated by
Light becomes light – a wave
of goodness shimmering
in the dark.

Ephesians 5:8-14

Sunday / 5

Your life is rare but
don't ration it. Rather,
pour out the rich aroma
in every room you reside.

John 12:1-8

Day 29 / Monday

Christt,
is a super massive
star sitting squarely
in space and time.

We
are dust caught
in the glory – happy
to spin around such
marvelous light.

John 12:20-33

Day 30 / Tuesday

Valley of bones dry
thirst for winds to blow,
pray for life to boldly rise
that Israel may know.

Tendon, muscle, skin
stretch and cover frame,
inspiration exhale
ignite a living flame.

Heaven's holy wind
from earth gracious flow,
sweep through human brittle bone,
Sower of seed now sow.

Ezekiel 37:1-14

Day 31 / Wednesday

This school has many
teachers, but only one lesson.
A true metric is the quality of
your tears.

Hebrews 5:5-10

Day 32 / Thursday

When you play around in the
past you miss God pushing
seas aside for his beloved.

Isaiah 43:16-21

Day 33 / Friday

Every good deed is a rung
in your ladder to heaven.
Congratulations, you're forty feet
off the ground – too bad
heaven is somewhere way past

Pluto.

Philippians 3:4B-14

Day 34 / Saturday

Through every alleyway and
underpass of the heart God
in shadow sneaks, writing his
secret name.

Jeremiah 31:33b-34

Sunday / 6 / Palm Sunday

If you keep quiet, then cats will
call to worship. Stones will sing
the psalms, plants will pass the
peace, bee's will buzz with
confession and that's just the
start. Don't wait 'till sloths start
sermonizing before you open
your mouth and praise, please.

Luke 19:28-40

Day 35 / Monday

No sword did Christ raise
that night. Only bread –

blessed,
broken,
given.

Luke 22:7-22

Day 36 / Tuesday

There is a bitter cup
we all must drink. See
the grimace on his
face.

Luke 22:39-53

Day 37 / Wednesday

Every loss is a seed.

Bury your loss,
water it with your tears,
wait patiently for the light.

Luke 22:54-65

Day 38 / Maundy Thursday

Here is a quick shot of poetry
to deliver something straight
and sweet to your soiled and
sad heart – from a pile of mud,
God will make a palace of
light.

Luke 22:7-8, 14-22

Day 39 / Good Friday

Of all things noble
you could have been dear tree,
never did you dream you'd be a
beam holding your bleeding
Maker.

Mark 15:25-39

Day 40 / Holy Saturday

So much depends upon
a real body broken,
soiled in red sorrow,
wrapped in white linen.

Luke 23:50-56

This poem was inspired by a
William Carlos Williams poem called
"XXII" – from *Spring and All* (1923)

Sunday / Easter

On Friday, death was hungry
and had a feast. On Saturday,
death was ill with something
sacred. On Sunday death was
sorry to have eaten that
rich meal so hastily.

Matthew 28:1-10